MARISSA MOSS

NURSE, SOLDIER, SPY

THE STORY OF SARAH EDMONDS, A CIVIL WAR HERO

JOHN HENDRIX

ABRAMS BOOKS FOR YOUNG READERS, NEW YORK

President Abraham Lincoln had just declared war on the Southern states seceding from the Union, and the new army needed men. When Frank Thompson saw a poster requesting recruits, he decided he would be one of them. Except Frank wasn't his real name. In fact, Frank wasn't a man. He was really Sarah Emma Edmonds.

3

Sarah was only nineteen, but she had already been dressing as a man for three years. Originally, she had cut her brown wavy hair and put on pants to escape a marriage arranged by her parents.

She had run away, crossing the border from Canada into the United States, trading a bridal gown for trousers, trading countries, without a single regret. Once she discovered the freedom of taking big strides unhindered by heavy skirts, and the freedom to travel when and where she wanted, she couldn't put a dress back on.

Now, as Frank Thompson, she joined the long line of men snaking around the Michigan courthouse, eager to give back to the country that had given her a new life.

When it was her turn, she leaned over for the pen, ready to sign on to the Union army.

"JUST A MOMENT THERE,"

the recruiter said.

Sarah froze. Could he tell she was a woman? How? She'd been fooling people for so long, she thought her disguise was perfect. Growing up on a farm, she'd learned to handle a gun and a horse. Even then, she'd put on her brother's homespun pants to hunt. So learning to walk, talk, eat, and gesture like a man had come easy to her. By now, it was a habit.

"I know you love your country," the man said kindly, "but you need to grow up a bit before you join the army." He looked at her peachy cheeks free of any sign of a whisker. "We aren't taking any sixteen-year-olds."

"But . . . ," Sarah protested, both relieved and frustrated.

"By the time you're old enough, son, this war will be over. Now go on home." The recruiter took the pen and passed it to the unshaven farmer behind her.

Sarah's ears burned red with shame. When the men left for basic training, the whole town of Flint, Michigan, saw them off. It was like a parade. Sarah cheered with everyone else, but she wanted desperately to be one of those going, not one of those staying behind and waving handkerchiefs in a teary good-bye.

A month later, she got her chance. More men were needed, and this time the recruiter only glanced at Sarah. "Another boy," he muttered, shaking his head. He'd already signed up a dozen gangly teenagers. This fresh-faced kid was no different. Sarah signed her name, Frank Thompson, with a firm flourish. She was now a private in Company F, Second Michigan Volunteer Infantry of the Army of the Potomac.

Frank could outshoot and outride many country boys, and was certainly more skilled than all the city folk. She felt at home in the army, living with a large group of men, practicing drills together, learning the discipline of a fighting force. She liked sharing a tent. Since the soldiers slept in their clothes, it didn't seem risky, but cozy. Frank loved the easy camaraderie and jokes, sharing stories and letters from back home.

She didn't even mind being teased. The other soldiers laughed at her small boots and called her

"OUR LITTLE WOMAN!"

Frank laughed louder than the rest of them at the nickname. If only they knew!

For the first time in years, Frank had friends—and work that really mattered. She was proud of what she was doing, first learning to be a soldier, then training as a nurse, which was something only men with the strongest stomachs did because of the long, draining hours and the horrors of surgery without anesthetic.

One bloody battle followed another. Sometimes the North won, sometimes the South, but always the soldiers lost, thousands of them dying or maimed.

Frank fought alongside her friends in the Battle of Bull Run and the Battle of Fair Oaks. She pulled wounded men from the battlefield, racing through minié balls and shells to save as many as possible.

During the Battle of Williamsburg, a fellow nurse yelled at her to help retrieve an officer who lay on the ground, groaning in pain. Frank heaved the colonel's limp body onto the cloth and grabbed the other end of the stretcher. The two nurses raced to the edge of the battlefield, where the doctors waited for the injured.

"Dr. Bonine," she called. "Over here! This man's a colonel!"

The doctor bent over the officer's still body.

"Is he dead?" Frank asked, sick at the thought of carrying a corpse instead of rescuing a soldier.

"He's breathing, but I don't know what's wrong." The doctor poked and prodded. "Where are you injured, sir? I don't see any mark. Are you hurt?" The question changed into a roar of accusation. "You, sir, are a fraud! Get up this instant and back into battle before I report you as a deserter!"

Without a word the colonel brushed himself off and strode away while Frank seethed. *No coward will fool me again,* she promised herself. *There are too many real soldiers who need my help.*

One late April night when the troops were preparing for the siege of Yorktown, Frank was making the rounds in the hospital tent when the regimental chaplain approached her.

"If you're willing, there's an important job I want to recommend you for. It's dangerous, but I wouldn't ask you if I didn't think you could do it."

More dangerous than fighting? Frank thought, but waited for the chaplain to explain.

"One of our best spies has been captured and killed." The chaplain pressed his long fingers together. "I think you're just the man to replace him. I'd like to give your name to the generals." He paused, looking intently at Frank's young, soft face. He'd seen the boy face the ugliest wounds without flinching, had seen him race through gunfire to rescue a wounded soldier. Still, he knew he was asking the nurse to take even greater risks as a spy.

"Will you do it?"

Frank didn't hesitate.

"I'M YOUR MAN!"

For her first mission, Frank decided to
disguise herself as a freed slave.

She knew that white men, especially Southerners, didn't look closely at black men. Slaves were even more invisible than old women, people who were looked *past*, not *at*. So she darkened her skin with silver nitrate, put on a wig and torn clothes, and headed off to the rebel lines just as the day was dawning.

In the darkened stillness, she crawled along the ground, stopping every time she heard a twig snap or a branch rustle.

When she thought she must have passed the sentries, she stood up on nervous legs, looking for the tents of the Confederate camp. She soon ran into a group of slaves bringing breakfast to the rebel pickets, the men who guarded the camp.

"Mind if I join you?" she asked. "I'm lookin' for work."

"We got work aplenty, if that's what you want." A skinny young boy offered her corn bread and coffee. Frank wolfed it down, nodding her thanks. But after she helped carry food to the pickets and followed the group back into camp, she wasn't sure what to do. The others knew exactly where to go and melted off to their assigned places. Which one should she follow, Frank wondered. Where would she learn the most?

OY! BELONG TO? WHY ARE YOU STANDIN' THERE, GAWKING?"

"I don't belong to no man," Frank said. "I'm headin' to Richmond to find work."

"As long as there's a Confederate army, y'all belong to SOMEONE!" the officer roared. "There'll be no free slaves so long as our hearts beat strong, and don't you forget it! Now go work on the fortifications if you don't want a whuppin'."

Frank gritted her teeth, but she did as she was told.

Frank followed the line of sweating black workers pushing gravel-filled wheelbarrows over a narrow plank to build up the earthworks facing the Union army. Frank was used to hard work, but by midday her palms were bloody and raw.

She almost tipped her wheelbarrow twice. Each time, another worker rushed over to help her. For now, all she could do was nod her thanks, but she was determined that she would find a way to repay her new friends.

While digging, wheeling, and heaping up gravel, Frank studied the layout of the rebel fortifications. She counted guns and noted logs that had been painted black and set up to look like cannons from a distance. When night fell, and everyone else was asleep, she took out the paper and pencil she'd hidden in her shoe and started to write what she remembered.

15   3" rifled cannon
18   4½" rifled cannon
29   32 pounders
21   42 pounders
23   8" Columbiads
11   9" Dahlgrens
13   10" Columbiads
14   10" mortars
7   8" Siege howitzers

After listing the weapons, she flipped over the paper to sketch the ramparts and mark where each gun stood. Footsteps clomped behind her, and she quickly folded the plan and stuck it back in its hiding place.

The next morning, her muscles were stiff and sore and her palms so raw she didn't see how she could manage the pickax. When she saw the slender boy with the friendly eyes again, this time filling buckets with water, she got an idea.

"You bringin' water to the troops?" she asked the boy.

"Uh-huh," he said, nodding his head.

"Would you mind tradin' jobs with me? I got no skin left on my hands. I'll give you thirty cents if you switch with me." Frank held out some coins.

The boy shook his head. "I can't use money. But I'll switch jobs, don't you worry."

Frank grinned. "I'll make it up to you, I promise."

Frank heaved up the heavy buckets and headed for a cluster of soldiers. As she filled canteens, she was surprised to recognize a tall, lanky peddler who came to the Union camp once a week, selling newspapers and stationery for letters home. He was busy describing the layout of the Union camp and its defenses.

"Well, I'll be," Frank muttered, sloshing water on the spy's leg.

"Hey, watch it there, dolt!" the fake peddler yelled.

Frank lowered her head. "Sorry, sorry," she said. And she really was sorry—sorry she couldn't rush back to the Union camp right then and tell the generals what she'd learned.

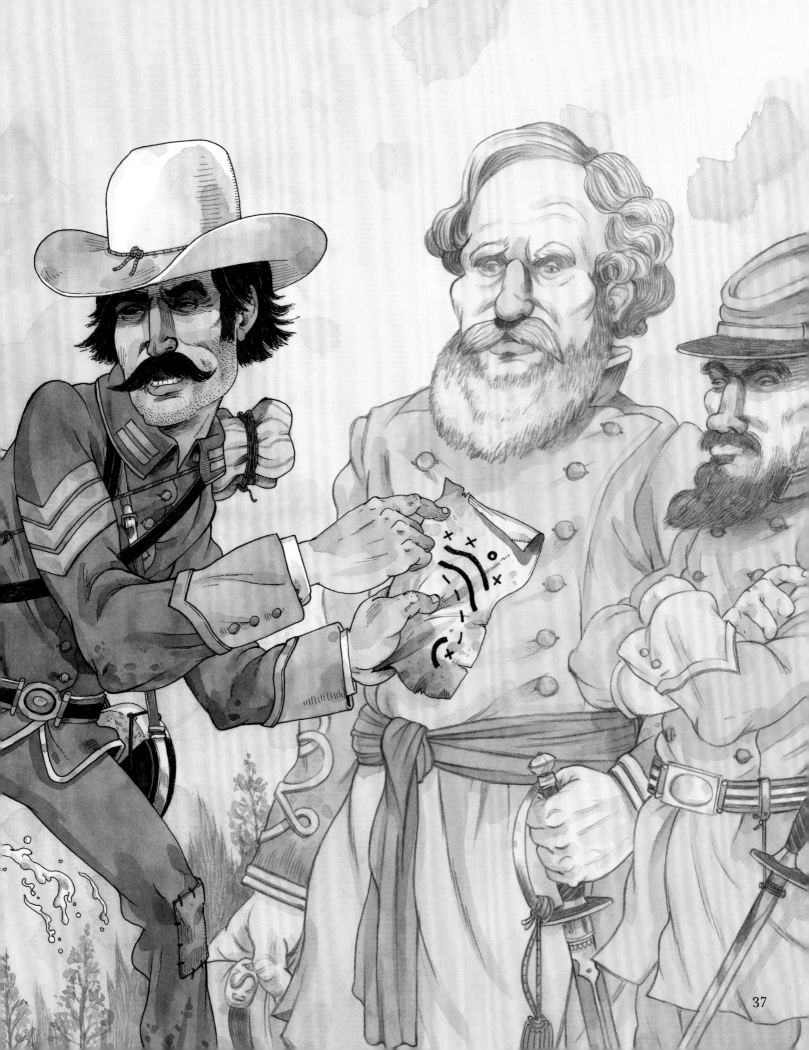

Frank waited until the sun set, and then she headed toward the pickets, hoping she could slip by a soldier if he nodded off or got distracted. The only thing to hide her was the darkness. She hadn't gone far, though, when a voice stopped her.

"YOU, T

HERE!"

Frank turned to face a thick-set officer. "Take this rifle and head for the picket post by the brambles. The guard was shot, so we need a replacement." The officer handed Frank a gun. "And don't you even think about shutting those eyes of yours!"

Frank headed off, surprised that the rebel would hand a weapon to a slave. Didn't he worry about a slave revolt? Later, she learned it was Confederate policy not to arm slaves, something this particular officer didn't seem to care about, luckily for her. Frank took her post and then kept on going. Once she got close to the Union pickets, she curled up on the ground to wait until morning.

As the sun rose, Frank took off her wig and waved it at the Union picket near her. Her hair felt cool and free in the morning breeze.

"IT'S PRIVATE

"Li

40

FRANK THOMPSON!"

"I don't care what yo' name is. Ya ain't comin' one step closer lessen' you got the password." The guard cocked his rifle and squinted down the barrel.

BERTY BELL."

Frank grinned, twirling the wig on her finger. The guard gaped, but lowered his gun. Frank must have made an odd sight, dressed in rags, with darkened skin and matted hair. She took long, easy strides, tired and hungry, but feeling strangely light inside. She opened the flap of the generals' tent, ready to report what she'd learned. Freedom, she knew, wasn't something to take for granted. It was something to fight for, to cherish.

And so long as her heart was beating strong, that's just what she would do.

AUTHOR'S NOTE

When I decided that I wanted to write about the Civil War, I wasn't sure how I would approach such a vast subject, so I started by looking at women and what roles they had played both in the North and the South. When I first came across the story of Sarah Emma Edmonds, it didn't sound particularly exciting, but I was intrigued enough to keep digging. The brief mention I'd found hinted at bigger possibilities, but I was completely astonished to learn the fascinating depths to her story. Not only was she the only woman I could find who had lived as a man before enlisting, but she was also the only woman who held the extraordinary range of positions she did—from nurse to spy to postmaster to general's orderly. When I discovered that she'd written about her experience, that I'd be able to learn about her life in her own words, that was it. I knew I had to write about her.

I relied on her own memoir, *Unsexed; or, the Female Soldier*, published in 1865; as well as Sylvia Dannett's *She Rode with the Generals; The Mysterious Private Thompson*, by Laura Leedy Gansler; *Where Duty Calls: The Story of Sarah Emma Edmonds, Soldier and Spy in the Union Army*, by Marilyn Seguin; and numerous books on women in the Civil War as well as on the Civil War in general.

Frank Thompson did repay the young slave who traded jobs with her in the Confederate camp. After one battle, she was tending to the wounded when she recognized the boy who had helped her. She made sure the doctor gave him special care before she went on to her next patient.

As a spy, Frank went on ten more missions, each time wearing a different disguise, changing from an old Irish woman to a Confederate soldier to a young Southern boy. She worked as a regimental mail carrier and a general's orderly, as well as a nurse, and fought in some of the biggest battles of the war, including the battles of Bull Run, Fair Oaks, and Fredericksburg.

Weakened by malaria and seriously wounded twice, Frank refused medical treatment for fear of being discovered as a woman. Finally, in 1863, she was so weak from a bout of malaria that she slipped out of camp, dressed herself as a woman, and as an ordinary civilian saw a doctor. Once her strength returned, she put her uniform back on and was on her way to rejoin her regiment when she saw a poster that stopped her in her tracks. Private Frank Thompson, it announced in large black letters, was a deserter from the Union army and should be shot on sight. That spelled the end of Frank's army career. She changed back into a dress, and although she would often wear pants, she never again took on a man's identity.

Two years later, Sarah Emma Edmonds finished her memoir, dedicated to the sick and wounded soldiers of the Army of the Potomac. Hundreds of women had disguised themselves as men and fought on both sides of the war, usually joining a husband, brother, or father. The newspapers often carried stories of their thrilling exploits, but none of the women had written a book. Sarah brought the manuscript to her old boss from her Bible-selling days when she had first arrived in the United States. If he was surprised that the Frank Thompson he'd hired was really a woman, he didn't show it. He was happy to see his most successful salesman again, and he published what became an instant bestseller, selling 175,000 copies in the first year. Sarah donated the entire proceeds to an organization helping Civil War veterans.

As a civilian, Sarah married a carpenter who was comfortable with her past. Together, they worked to improve the lives of African Americans and veterans. First they managed an orphanage built for children whose African American fathers had died in the Civil War. Then she and her husband worked to build a home for disabled veterans. Needing money for both good causes, she applied for a pension and to have her dishonorable discharge changed to an honorable one.

After visiting many of the soldiers she had fought alongside, she sent to Congress their written testimonials about her exceptional service and her identity, proving that Sarah Emma Edmonds Seelye (her married name) and Frank Thompson were one and the same person.

It took several years and two different acts of Congress, but in 1886 and again in 1889, Sarah Emma Edmonds Seelye became the first and only woman to be recognized as a veteran of the Civil War with an honorable discharge and to receive a pension and back pay for her service. She was also the only woman invited to join the Grand Army of the Republic (GAR), the association for Civil War veterans of the Union army. When she went to her first reunion, in April 1897, she was enthusiastically welcomed by her fellow veterans, many of whom told fond stories about "Frank." When she died in 1898, her coffin was carried by a delegation of the veterans' association, and a GAR chaplain performed the service. Sarah Emma Edmonds Seelye was the only woman to be buried in a military cemetery, in a plot reserved for Civil War veterans. Her tombstone simply records her name and the title "Nurse," the one she was most proud of, but a quote from her memoir would have made a fitting inscription:

"I am naturally fond of adventure, a little ambitious, and a good deal romantic—but patriotism was the true secret of my success."

ARTIST'S NOTE

The first job of any illustrator is to communicate—with both clarity and poetry. Images provide context and information, but they should also amplify the text in unexpected ways. This is the third book I've illustrated that is set in the years surrounding the Civil War. But even with this experience, I have to collect lots of visual resources before I can start drawing a book like this. These include books and image collections, exhibitions I've visited, and my own photographs. But visual resources can come from anywhere. In fact, when I was touring Harpers Ferry, West Virginia, I bought a kid's Civil War coloring book that actually became a very useful guide to soldiers' uniforms!

Some of the other items I had to research and practice drawing included Union and Confederate equipment, how the soldiers' tents looked on the inside, and even how fences were constructed. And let me tell you, I can draw a split-rail log fence in my sleep! But even before all these details, there was Sarah Emma Edmonds herself. There are only a few images that still exist of Sarah. So I had to guess at much of her clothes, her posture, and her freckles. She needed to look different from the other characters in the book, but still appear strong and confident in her abilities.

One note about the hand-drawn typography: Much of the illustrated letterforms are drawn from actual broadside posters of the era that were made with wooden type on a printing press. Some of these typefaces came from posters announcing war and others announcing concerts. These posters, in some cases composed of a dozen individual typefaces, endure as classic visual examples of the time.

GLOSSARY

Abraham Lincoln: The sixteenth president of the United States, from March 1861 until his assassination in April 1865. He led the country through the Civil War with the Southern states, preserving the government and helping to free African Americans from slavery.

Anesthetic: A medicine that eliminates or minimizes the experience of pain

The Civil War (1861–1865): The war fought on American soil between opposing sides of the nation's citizens. Eleven Southern states seceded from the United States (the Union) and formed a separate nation, the Confederate States of America, also known as "the Confederacy." They fought against the United States, which was supported by all the free states (where slavery had been abolished) and by five slave states that became known as the Border States.

Confederate: A Southern soldier, or something having to do with the Confederate States of America

Deserter: A soldier who runs away from fighting or military service without plans to return

Dolt: A stupid person (an insult)

Drills: Exercises that soldiers do to prepare for battle

Earthworks: Fortifications made by piling up walls of soil

Fortifications: Walls made of earth, stone, or wood to protect soldiers in camp

Fraud: A person who is not who she or he pretends to be

Generals: Officers in the army who hold the highest rank and lead soldiers into battle

Minié ball: Also called a minnie ball, a type of bullet used in rifles at the time of the Civil War

The North: The group of states that fought to preserve the Union and to keep the United States as one country during the Civil War. This group included the northern states of Connecticut, Maine, Massachusetts, New Hampshire, New Jersey, New York, Pennsylvania, Rhode Island, and Vermont. Many states and territories in the West and Midwest (California, Colorado, Illinois, Indiana, Iowa, Kansas, Michigan, Minnesota, Nebraska, Nevada [which became a state during the war], New Mexico, Ohio, Oregon, Utah, Washington, and Wisconsin) also fought on the side of the North. The western part of Virginia broke away from that state to fight for the Union and became a separate state called West Virginia. West Virginia, Delaware, Maryland, Kentucky, and Missouri were called the Border States. They did not leave the Union and join the South, but some parts of these states were sympathetic to the Confederacy.

Password: A word or phrase that is used to keep enemies from sneaking into camp. A person who doesn't know it may be a spy or an enemy soldier. The right word or phrase is like a key that lets a person in.

Peddler: A merchant who travels to sell his goods, or sells his goods on the street

Pickets: Another name for sentries. Pickets stand guard at the outer edges of camp.

Post: A place a soldier is put to stand guard

Private: The lowest rank in the army; a regular foot soldier

Ramparts: The tops of fortifications, sometimes wide enough that soldiers can walk on them

Rebel: A Confederate soldier

Recruits: Newly enlisted members of the army

Regimental chaplain: A preacher who leads religious services for soldiers

Sentries: Soldiers who guard the camp

Shells: Explosive devices shot from cannons and used as artillery weapons

Silver nitrate: A chemical compound that turns skin dark and was often used for disguise

The South: The slave-owning states that seceded from the United States and formed a separate nation called the Confederate States of America. They were Alabama, Arkansas, Florida, Georgia, Louisiana, Mississippi, North Carolina, South Carolina, Tennessee, Texas, and Virginia.

Spy: A person (often in disguise) who sneaks into enemy territory to obtain information and bring that information back to their side in a war

The Union: The name of the United States during the Civil War

AUTHOR'S BIBLIOGRAPHY

Abbott, Diane L., and Kristoffer Gair. *Honor Unbound*. Dallas: Hamilton Books, 2004.

Blanton, DeAnne and Lauren Cook. *They Fought Like Demons: Women Soldiers in the American Civil War*. New York: Vintage, 2003.

Dannett, Sylvia G. L. *She Rode with the Generals: The True and Incredible Story of Sarah Emma Seelye, Alias Franklin Thompson*. Edinburgh, NY: T. Nelson, 1960.

Edmonds, Sarah Emma. *Unsexed; or, the Female Soldier*. Later published as *Nurse and Spy in the Union Army: Comprising the Adventures and Experiences of a Woman in Hospitals, Camps, and Battle-Fields*. Hartford: Williams, 1865.

Emert, Phyllis Raybin, ed. *Women in the Civil War: Warriors, Patriots, Nurses, and Spies*. Boston: History Compass, 2008.

Gansler, Laura Leedy. *The Mysterious Private Thompson: The Double Life of Sarah Emma Edmonds, Civil War Soldier*. Lincoln: Bison Books, 2007.

Hall, Richard. *Women on the Civil War Battlefront*. Lawrence: University Press of Kansas, 2006.

Hancock, Cornelia. *Letters of a Civil War Nurse*. Lincoln: Bison Books, 1998.

Hancock, Cornelia. *South after Gettysburg: Letters of Cornelia Hancock from the Army of the Potomac, 1863–1865*. New York: T. Y. Crowell Co., 1956.

Harper, Judith E. *Women During the Civil War: An Encyclopedia*. New York: Routledge, 2007.

Markle, Donald E. *Spies and Spymasters of the Civil War*. New York: Barnes & Noble Books, 1998.

Massey, Mary Elizabeth. *Women in the Civil War*. Introduction to the Bison Book edition by Jean Berlin. Lincoln: University of Nebraska Press, 1994.

Schultz, Jane E. *Women at the Front: Hospital Workers in Civil War America*. Chapel Hill: University of North Carolina Press, 2007.

Seguin, Marilyn. *Where Duty Calls: The Story of Sarah Emma Edmonds, Soldier and Spy in the Union Army*. Boston: Branden Pub. Co., 1999.

Tsui, Bonnie. *She Went to the Field: Women Soldiers of the Civil War*. Guilford, CT: TwoDot, 2006.

ARTIST'S BIBLIOGRAPHY

Copeland, Peter F. *Story of the Civil War Coloring Book*. New York: Dover Publications, 1991.

Copeland, Peter F. *The Story of the Underground Railroad*. New York: Dover Publications, 2000.

Editors of Time-Life Books. *Soldier Life*. Alexandria, VA: Time-Life Books, 1996.

Langellier, John P. *Terrible, Swift Sword: Union Artillery, Cavalry, and Infantry, 1861–1865*. Philadelphia: Chelsea House Publishers, 2000.

Miller, William J., and Brian C. Pohanka. *An Illustrated History of the Civil War: Images of an American Tragedy*. Alexandria, VA: Time-Life Books, 2000.

Scott, John Anthony. *The Story of America: A National Geographic Picture Atlas*. Washington, D.C.: National Geographic Society, 1992.

Stanchak, John. *Civil War*. New York: Dorling Kindersley Pub., 2000.

SARAH EMMA EDMONDS

SARAH EMMA EDMONDS
DISGUISED
AS FRANK THOMPSON

INDEX

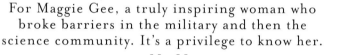

For Maggie Gee, a truly inspiring woman who broke barriers in the military and then the science community. It's a privilege to know her.
—M. M.

To Annie, my little girl
—J. H.

The illustrations in this book were made with pen and ink
with fluid acrylic washes on Strathmore Velum Bristol.

Library of Congress Cataloging-in-Publication Data

Moss, Marissa.
Nurse, soldier, spy : The story of Sarah Edmonds, a Civil War hero / by Marissa Moss; illustrated by John Hendrix.
p. cm.
ISBN 978-0-8109-9735-6 (alk. paper)
1. Edmonds, S. Emma E. (Sarah Emma Evelyn), 1841–1898—Juvenile literature. 2. United States—History—Civil War,
1861–1865—Participation, Female—Juvenile literature. 3. United States—History—Civil War, 1861–1865—Women—Juvenile literature.
4. United States—History—Civil War, 1861–1865—Secret service—Juvenile literature. 5. Nurses—United States—Biography—Juvenile literature.
6. Women soldiers—United States—Biography—Juvenile literature. 7. Soldiers—United States—Biography—Juvenile literature. 8. Women spies—
United States—Biography—Juvenile literature. 9. Spies—United States—Biography—Juvenile literature. I. Hendrix, John, 1976– II. Title.
E608.E235M67 2011
973.7092—dc22
[B]
2010023171

Text copyright © 2011 Marissa Moss
Illustrations copyright © 2011 John Hendrix
Book design by Chad W. Beckerman and John Hendrix

ABRAMS
THE ART OF BOOKS SINCE 1949

115 West 18th Street
New York, NY 10011
www.abramsbooks.com